GOD'S LITTLE INS...

CLASS OF 2007

MW00716052

HONOR HB BOOKS

Inspiration and Motivation for the Seasons of Life

COOK COMMUNICATIONS MINISTRIES   Colorado Springs, Colorado   •   Paris, Ontario
KINGSWAY COMMUNICATIONS LTD   Eastbourne, England

Honor® is an imprint of
Cook Communications Ministries, Colorado Springs, CO 80918
Cook Communications, Paris, Ontario
Kingsway Communications, Eastbourne, England

God's Little Instruction Book for the Class of 2007

Cover Design: BMB Design

First printing, 2006
Printed in Canada

1 2 3 4 5 6 Printing/Year 10 09 08 07 06

ISBN-13: 978-1-56292-735-6
ISBN-10: 1-56292-735-3

INTRODUCTION

Congratulations! As a member of the Class of 2007, you have the privilege and responsibility of being part of the most important group of people on earth—those who will be setting the pace, establishing the values, and initiating the changes for a world that suddenly finds itself face-to-face with the future.

Like every generation that has come before, you will encounter enormous challenges as well as amazing opportunities. And you are bound to find that you will be confronted with difficult questions and complex issues for which there are no precedents. You will truly be going where no one has gone before—except God! How will you find the answers you need?

In *God's Little Instruction Book for the Class of 2007*, we at Honor Books offer you God's timeless wisdom taken from the one book that will never be obsolete—the Bible. We hope the truths presented in these pages will serve as cherished resources for you as you launch out into the depths of human possibility and potential.

The future belongs to those who believe in the beauty of their dreams.

May he give you the desire of your heart and make all your plans succeed.

PSALM 20:4

To accomplish great things we must not only act, but also dream; not only plan, but also believe.

All things are possible to him that believeth.

MARK 9:23 KJV

5

The journey of a thousand miles begins with one step.

God did not give us a spirit of timidity,
but a spirit of power, of love and of self-discipline.

2 TIMOTHY 1:7

Laughter gives us distance. It allows us to step back from an event, deal with it, and then move on.

Our light affliction, which is but for a moment, worketh for us a far more exceeding and eternal weight of glory.

2 CORINTHIANS 4:17 KJV

God is the God of promise.
He keeps His word, even when
that seems impossible; even when
the circumstances seem to
point to the opposite.

What I have said, that will I bring about; what I have planned, that will I do.
Isaiah 46:11

Pure and simple, faith not lived every day is not faith; it is facade.

If you do not stand firm in your faith, you will not stand at all.

ISAIAH 7:9

9

Believe in yourself! Have faith in your abilities! Without a humble but reasonable confidence in your own powers, you cannot be successful or happy.

There's nothing better than being wise, knowing how to interpret the meaning of life. Wisdom puts light in the eyes, and gives gentleness to words and manners.

ECCLESIASTES 8:1 MSG

CLASS OF 2007

Fear and worry are interest paid in advance on something you may never own.

Do not worry about your life, what you will eat or drink; or about your body, what you will wear.

Matthew 6:25

CLASS OF
2007

11

No sin is small.

I am troubled by my sin.
PSALM 38:18

Guts: Grace under pressure.

We have this hope as an anchor for the soul, firm and secure.

HEBREWS 6:19

The only way to discover the limits of the possible is to go beyond them into the impossible.

*Jesus said unto him, If thou canst believe,
all things are possible to him that believeth.*

MARK 9:23 KJV

14

God's Little Instruction Book

We are all faced with a series of great opportunities brilliantly disguised as impossible situations.

Fight the good fight of the faith. Take hold of the eternal life to which you were called when you made your good confession in the presence of many witnesses.

1 TIMOTHY 6:12

15

Smart is believing half of what you hear; brilliant is knowing which half to believe.

Wisdom and truth will enter the very center of your being, filling your life with joy.

Proverbs 2:10 TLB

Speak when you are angry—
and you will make the best speech
you'll ever regret.

Watch your words and hold your tongue; you'll save yourself a lot of grief.
PROVERBS 21:23 MSG

17

Never, for fear of feeble man, restrain your witness.

If anyone publicly acknowledges me as his friend, I will openly acknowledge him as my friend before my father in heaven.

Matthew 10:32 tlb

When the character of a man is not clear to you, look at his friends.

A righteous man is cautious in friendship.

PROVERBS 12:26

We need to pay more attention to how we treat people than to how they treat us.

You must love others as much as you love yourself.

MARK 12:31 TLB

20

Fire is the test of gold; adversity, of strong men.

Blessed is the man who perseveres under trial, because when he has stood the test, he will receive the crown of life that God has promised to those who love him.

JAMES 1:12

CLASS OF 2007

21

Things are not always what they seem.

The LORD does not look at the things man looks at. Man looks at the outward appearance, but the LORD looks at the heart.

1 SAMUEL 16:7

CLASS OF 2007

Death is more universal than life; every man dies, not every man lives.

I have come that they may have life, and have it to the full.

John 10:10

23

Wise men talk because they have something to say; fools because they have to say something.

The mouth of the righteous man utters wisdom, and his tongue speaks what is just.

PSALM 37:30

24

The only thing we have to fear is fear itself.

God is our refuge and strength, an ever-present help in trouble.
Therefore we will not fear.

PSALM 46:1–2

The answer is always in God.

Seek first his kingdom and his righteousness, and all these things will be given to you as well.

MATTHEW 6:33

When one door closes, another door opens.

Let your eyes look straight ahead, fix your gaze directly before you.

PROVERBS 4:25

Hope awakens *courage*. He who can implant *courage* in the human soul is the best physician.

But Christ is faithful as a son over God's house.
And we are his house, if we hold on to our courage
and the hope of which we boast.

HEBREWS 3:6

To have faith is to believe the task ahead of us is never as great as the power behind us.

Now to him who is able to do immeasurably more than all we ask or imagine, according to his power that is at work within us.

EPHESIANS 3:20

CLASS OF
2007

Every oak tree started out as a couple of nuts who stood their ground.

*My dear brothers, stand firm. Let nothing move you.
Always give yourselves fully to the work of the Lord,
because you know that your labor in the Lord is not in vain.*

1 CORINTHIANS 15:58

There can be no such thing as a necessary evil. For if a thing is really necessary, it cannot be an evil, and if it is an evil, it is not necessary.

This is what the LORD says: "Stand at the crossroads and look;
ask for the ancient paths, ask where the good way is, and walk in it,
and you will find rest for your souls."

JEREMIAH 6:16

31

Effort only fully releases its reward after a person refuses to quit.

Don't quit in hard times; pray all the harder.

ROMANS 12:12 MSG

God's Little Instruction Book

I try to avoid looking forward or backward and try to keep looking upward.

I have set the LORD always before me.
Because he is at my right hand, I will not be shaken.

PSALM 16:8

33

Courage is fear that has said its prayers.

I have told you these things, so that in me you may have peace. In this world you will have trouble. But take heart! I have overcome the world.

JOHN 16:33

CLASS OF 2007

When we long for life without difficulties, remind us that oaks grow strong in contrary winds and diamonds are made under pressure.

Perseverance must finish its work so that you may be mature and complete, not lacking anything.

JAMES 1:4

It is the heart which perceives God and not the reason.

Keep thy heart with all diligence; for out of it are the issues of life.

PROVERBS 4:23 KJV

36

God will not demand more from you than you can do. Whatever God asks of you, He will give you the strength to do.

So now, go. I am sending you to Pharaoh to bring my people the Israelites out of Egypt.

EXODUS 3:10

37

Have courage for the great sorrows of life and patience for the small ones, and when you have laboriously accomplished your daily task, go to sleep in peace. God is awake.

He will not let your foot slip—he who watches over you will not slumber.

PSALM 121:3

Five great enemies to peace: greed, ambition, envy, anger, and pride.

The LORD blesses his people with peace.

PSALM 29:11

39

Life affords no greater pleasure than overcoming obstacles.

I can do everything through him [Christ] who gives me strength.

PHILIPPIANS 4:13

What is our relationship to God? … The position that we stand in to him is that of a son. Adam is the father of our bodies, and God is the father of our spirits.

Here's how we can be sure that we know God in the right way: Keep his commandments.

1 JOHN 2:3 MSG

41

The trouble with our times is that the future is not what it used to be.

We fix our eyes not on what is seen, but on what is unseen. For what is seen is temporary, but what is unseen is eternal.

2 CORINTHIANS 4:18

42

It is later
than you think.

The night is far spent, the day is at hand: let us therefore cast off the works of darkness, and let us put on the armour of light.

ROMANS 13:12 KJV

43

A ship in harbor is safe, but that is not what ships are built for.

You are the world's light—a city on a hill, glowing in the night for all to see. Don't hide your light!

MATTHEW 5:14–15 TLB

44

Living in the moment brings you a sense of reverence for all of life's blessings.

So don't be anxious about tomorrow.
God will take care of your tomorrow too.
Live one day at a time.

MATTHEW 6:34 TLB

45

Wisdom is the combination of honesty and knowledge applied through experience.

Teach us to number our days aright, that we may gain a heart of wisdom.

PSALM 90:12

46

God does not love us because we are valuable. We are valuable because God loves us.

The LORD delights in those who fear him, who put their hope in his unfailing love.

PSALM 147:11

47

The world is governed more by appearance than realities.

These are a shadow of the things that were to come; the reality, however, is found in Christ.

COLOSSIANS 2:17

48

You can tell the character of every man when you see how he receives praise.

God resisteth the proud, but giveth grace unto the humble.

JAMES 4:6 KJV

49

The goal of life is to find out God's will and to do it.

Just tell me what to do and I will do it, Lord.
As long as I live I'll wholeheartedly obey.

PSALM 119:33–34 TLB

Life can only be understood backwards, but it must be lived forwards.

This is what the LORD says—your Redeemer, the Holy One of Israel:
"I am the LORD your God, who teaches you what is best for you,
who directs you in the way you should go."

ISAIAH 48:17

It is better to have a permanent income than to be fascinating.

Lazy hands make a man poor, but diligent hands bring wealth.

PROVERBS 10:4

Men are not against you; they are merely for themselves.

Bear with each other and forgive whatever grievances you may have against one another. Forgive as the Lord forgave you.

COLOSSIANS 3:13

CLASS OF 2007

53

Life is a lot like tennis—the one who can serve the best seldom loses.

As we have opportunity, let us do good to all people.

GALATIANS 6:10

54

Life is my college. May I graduate well and earn some honors!

Show me your ways, O LORD, teach me your paths.

PSALM 25:4

Don't allow the future to scare you.

Whoever trusts in the LORD is kept safe.

PROVERBS 29:25

Great men are little men expanded; great lives are ordinary lives intensified.

Those who have served well gain an excellent standing and great assurance in their faith in Christ Jesus.

1 Timothy 3:13

57

The greater part of our happiness depends on our disposition and not our circumstances.

I know how to live on almost nothing or with everything. I have learned the secret of contentment in every situation.

PHILIPPIANS 4:12 TLB

Give light, and the darkness will disappear of itself.

*God saw that the light was good,
and He separated the light from the darkness.*

GENESIS 1:4

Take time to deliberate, but when the time for action arrives, stop thinking and go on.

Rise up; this matter is in your hands.
We will support you, so take courage and do it.

EZRA 10:4

Do not borrow trouble by dreading tomorrow. It is the dark menace of the future that makes cowards of us all.

He will command his angels concerning you to guard you in all your ways.
PSALM 91:11

61

Who lives in fear will never be a free man.

The LORD is with me; I will not be afraid.

PSALM 118:6

Faith is not belief without proof, but trust without reservations.

As for God, his way is perfect: the word of the LORD is tried: he is a buckler to all those that trust in him.

PSALM 18:30 KJV

63

Think of these things: whence you came, where you are going, and to whom you must account.

So then every one of us shall give account of himself to God.
ROMANS 14:12 KJV

64

Talk is cheap because supply exceeds demand.

He that hath knowledge spareth his words.

PROVERBS 17:27 KJV

To speak painful truth through loving words is friendship.

Faithful are the wounds of a friend.

PROVERBS 27:6 KJV

True wealth is living with passion and purpose.

Delight thyself also in the LORD: and he shall give thee the desires of thine heart.

PSALM 37:4 KJV

Blessed are those who see the hand of God in the haphazard, inexplicable, and seemingly senseless circumstances of life.

I am with you and will watch over you wherever you go.

GENESIS 28:15

68

From the errors of others, a wise man corrects his own.

Those who are wise will shine like the brightness of the heavens.

DANIEL 12:3

CLASS OF 2007

Thoughts lead on to purposes;
purposes go forth in action; actions
form habits; habits decide character;
and character fixes our destiny.

*The purposes of a man's heart are deep waters, but
a man of understanding draws them out.*

PROVERBS 20:5

Without prayer, we return to our own ability rather than to God.

I am glad to boast about how weak I am; I am glad to be a living demonstration of Christ's power, instead of showing off my own power and abilities.

2 CORINTHIANS 12:9 TLB

God dwells in eternity,
but time dwells in God.
He has already lived all our
tomorrows as He has lived
all our yesterdays.

Surely I [God] am with you always, to the very end of the age.
MATTHEW 28:20

72

Some never get started on their destiny because they cannot humble themselves to learn, grow, and change.

Do not think of yourself more highly than you ought.

ROMANS 12:3

73

Let your words be the genuine picture of your heart.

So he fed them according to the integrity of his heart; and guided them by the skilfulness of his hands.

PSALM 78:72 KJV

Do all the good you can, …
in all the ways you can, …
at all the times you can,
to all the people you can,
as long as ever you can.

*Do not forget to do good and to share with others,
for with such sacrifices God is pleased.*

HEBREWS 13:16

CLASS OF 2007

Make your life a mission— not an intermission.

Serve wholeheartedly, as if you were serving the Lord, not men.
EPHESIANS 6:7

One must always have one's boots on and be ready to go.

You also must be ready, because the Son of Man will come at an hour when you do not expect him.

LUKE 12:40

77

Every man is a missionary, now and forever, for good or for evil, whether he intends or designs it or not.

I have set before you life and death, blessing and cursing: therefore choose life.
DEUTERONOMY 30:19 KJV

CLASS OF 2007

It often happens that those of whom we speak least on earth are best known in heaven.

You are a chosen people, a royal priesthood, a holy nation, a people belonging to God, that you may declare the praises of him who called you out of darkness into his wonderful light.

1 PETER 2:9

Make haste slowly.

If from there you seek the LORD your God, you will find him if you look for him with all your heart and with all your soul.

DEUTERONOMY 4:29

Out of debt, out of danger.

Give everyone what you owe him…. Let no debt remain outstanding.

ROMANS 13:7–8

Snuggle in God's arms. When you are hurting, when you feel lonely, left out, let Him cradle you, comfort you, reassure you of His all-sufficient power and love.

Staying right at the center of God's love, keeping your arms open and outstretched, ready for the mercy of our Master, Jesus Christ. This is the unending life, the real life!

JUDE V. 21 MSG

I am an old man and have known a
great many troubles, but most
of them never happened.

I will lie down and sleep in peace, for you alone, O LORD, make me dwell in safety.

PSALM 4:8

Happiness depends on what happens; joy does not.

You have made known to me the path of life; you will fill me with joy in your presence, with eternal pleasures at your right hand.

PSALM 16:11

Look upon your chastening as God's chariots sent to carry your soul into the high places of spiritual achievement.

As many as I love, I rebuke and chasten: be zealous therefore, and repent.

REVELATION 3:19 KJV

85

God made the world round, so we would never be able to see too far down the road.

"For I know the plans I have for you," declares the LORD, *"plans to prosper you and not to harm you, plans to give you hope and a future."*

JEREMIAH 29:11

CLASS OF 2007

The most revolutionary statement in history is "Love thy enemy."

Love your enemies! Pray for those who persecute you! In that way, you will be acting as true children of your Father in heaven. For he gives his sunlight to both the evil and the good, and he sends rain on the just and on the unjust, too.

MATTHEW 5:44–45 NLT

87

Peace is not an absence of war;
it is a virtue, a state of mind,
a disposition for benevolence,
confidence, and justice.

Seek peace and pursue it.

PSALM 34:14

88

Thanksgiving is the language of heaven, and we had better start to learn it if we are not to be mere dumb aliens there.

For every creature of God is good, and nothing to be refused, if it be received with thanksgiving.

1 TIMOTHY 4:4 KJV

89

Within your heart
Keep one still, secret spot
Where dreams may go
And, sheltered so,
May thrive and grow.

Above all else, guard your heart, for it is the wellspring of life.

PROVERBS 4:23

90

God's investment in us is so great He could not possibly abandon us.

The LORD appeared to us in the past, saying: "I have loved you with an everlasting love; I have drawn you with loving-kindness."

JEREMIAH 31:3

Blessed is the man who finds out which way God is moving and then gets going in the same direction.

Whether you turn to the right or to the left, your ears will hear a voice behind you, saying, "This is the way; walk in it."

ISAIAH 30:21

92

Trust in yourself and you are doomed to disappointment, but trust in God and you are never to be confounded in time or eternity.

Guard my life, for I am devoted to you. You are my God;
save your servant who trusts in you.

PSALM 86:2

Debt is the worst poverty.

The borrower is servant to the lender.

PROVERBS 22:7

CLASS OF 2007

We can believe what we choose. We are answerable for what we choose to believe.

He that cometh to God must believe that he is, and that he is a rewarder of them that diligently seek him.

HEBREWS 11:6 KJV

CLASS OF
2007

95

The mark of a man is how he treats a person who can be of no possible use to him.

In everything you do, put God first, and he will direct you and crown your efforts with success.

PROVERBS 3:6 TLB

96

CLASS OF 2007

Fear defeats more people than any other one thing in the world.

Perfect love drives out fear.

1 JOHN 4:18

There is no music in rest, but there is the making of music in it.

Are you tired? Worn out? Burned out on religion? Come to me. Get away with me and you'll recover your life. I'll show you how to take a real rest.

MATTHEW 11:28 MSG

Never fear shadows. They simply mean there's light shining somewhere.

Yea, though I walk through the valley of the shadow of death,
I will fear no evil: for thou art with me.

PSALM 23:4 KJV

CLASS OF 2007

99

He who waits to do a great deal of good at once will never do anything.

*Finally, be ye all of one mind, having compassion one of another;
love as brethren, be pitiful, be courteous.*

1 PETER 3:8 KJV

The cure for fear is faith.

I sought the LORD, and he answered me; he delivered me from all my fears.

PSALM 34:4

Give your problems to God; he will be up all night anyway.

[Even] the very hairs on your head are all numbered. So don't be afraid;
you are more valuable to him than a whole flock of sparrows.

LUKE 12:7 NLT

102

Thanksgiving is good but thanks-living is better.

Thanks be to God! He gives us the victory through our Lord Jesus Christ.

1 CORINTHIANS 15:57

103

All I have seen teaches me to trust the creator for all I have not seen.

I will say of the Lord, "He is my refuge and my fortress, my God, in whom I trust."

PSALM 91:2

CLASS OF 2007

Any definition of a successful life must include serving others.

He that is the greatest among you shall be your servant.
MATTHEW 23:11 KJV

God never put anyone in a place too small to grow in.

Give thanks in all circumstances, for this is God's will for you in Christ Jesus.

1 THESSALONIANS 5:18

Act boldly and unseen forces will come to your aid.

We have the Lord our God to fight our battles for us!

2 CHRONICLES 32:8 TLB

The goal of a virtuous life is to become like God.

Cheerfully pleasing God is the main thing, and that's what we aim to do, regardless of our conditions.

2 CORINTHIANS 5:9 MSG

Pray often, for prayer is a shield to the soul, a sacrifice to God, and a scourge for Satan.

The prayer of a righteous man is powerful and effective.

JAMES 5:16

109

The essence of temptation is the invitation to live independently of God.

I am the vine; you are the branches. If a man remains in me and I in him, he will bear much fruit; apart from me you can do nothing.

JOHN 15:5

What we call adversity, God calls opportunity.

Rise up; this matter is in your hands.
We will support you, so take courage and do it.

Ezra 10:4

Learn the luxury of doing good.

Do not withhold good from those who deserve it when it is in your power to act.

PROVERBS 3:27

112

Every job is a self-portrait of the person who does it. Autograph your work with excellence.

Praise him for his mighty acts: praise him according to his excellent greatness.
PSALM 150:2 KJV

113

Truth, like surgery, may hurt, but it cures.

Speaking the truth in love, we will in all things grow up into him who is the Head, that is, Christ.

EPHESIANS 4:15

The capacity to care gives life its deepest significance.

Carry each other's burdens, and in this way you will fulfill the law of Christ.

GALATIANS 6:2

A community is like a ship; everyone ought to be prepared to take the helm.

You can develop a healthy, robust community that lives right with God and enjoy its results only if you do the hard work of getting along with each other, treating each other with dignity and honor.

JAMES 3:18 MSG

116

God loves each of us as if there were only one of us.

Christ's love compels us, because we are convinced that one died for all.

2 CORINTHIANS 5:14

It is amidst great perils that we see brave hearts.

I will not fear the tens of thousands drawn up against me on every side.

PSALM 3:6

118

The mind grows by what it feeds on.

The mind controlled by the Spirit is life and peace.

ROMANS 8:6

A smooth sea never made a skilled mariner.

The LORD liveth, who hath redeemed my soul out of all adversity.

2 SAMUEL 4:9 KJV

Your talent is God's gift to you. What you do with it is your gift back to God.

Every good and perfect gift is from above, coming down from the Father of the heavenly lights.

JAMES 1:17

Giving is the secret to a healthy life. Not necessarily money, but whatever a man has of encouragement and sympathy and understanding.

It is more blessed to give than to receive.
ACTS 20:35

122

Call on God, but row away from the rocks.

Wisdom and good judgment live together, for wisdom knows where to discover knowledge and understanding.

PROVERBS 8:12 TLB

He became what we are to make us what he is.

We ... are being transformed into his likeness with ever-increasing glory.

2 CORINTHIANS 3:18

124

Faithfulness in little things is a big thing.

Great is his faithfulness; his lovingkindness begins afresh each day.

LAMENTATIONS 3:23 TLB

You don't have to lie awake nights to succeed— just stay awake days.

*Take up your positions; stand firm and see the deliverance the L*ORD *will give you.*

2 CHRONICLES 20:17

126

Success consists of getting up more times than you fall.

I can do everything through him who gives me strength.
PHILIPPIANS 4:13

I am convinced that faith sometimes means knowing God can whether or not he does.

If we are thrown into the blazing furnace, the God we serve is able to save us from it.... But even if he does not, we want you to know, O king, that we will not serve your gods.

DANIEL 3:17–18

128

The stars are constantly shining, but often we do not see them until the dark hours.

My help comes from the LORD, the Maker of heaven and earth.
PSALM 121:2

129

It is far better for a man to see his own faults, than for anyone else to see them.

Search me, O God, and know my heart; test my thoughts.
Point out anything you find in me that makes you sad.

PSALMS 139:23–24 TLB

I have decided to stick with love. Hate is too great a burden to bear.

Do everything in love.

1 CORINTHIANS 16:14

131

At the height of laughter, the universe is flung into a kaleidoscope of new possibilities.

He will yet fill your mouth with laughter and your lips with shouts of joy.

JOB 8:21

Few things are impossible to
diligence and skill. Great works
are performed, not by strength,
but perseverance.

*We want each of you to show this same diligence to the very end,
in order to make your hope sure.*

HEBREWS 6:11

Learn from yesterday; live for today; hope for tomorrow.

We have this hope as an anchor for the soul, firm and secure.

HEBREWS 6:19

Only one thing has to change for us
to know happiness in our lives:
where we focus our attention.

Jesus said, "Love the Lord your God with all your passion
and prayer and intelligence."

MATTHEW 22:37 MSG

135

There are at least four things you can do with your hands. You can wring them in despair, fold them in idleness, clench them in anger, or use them to help someone.

She opens her arms to the poor and extends her hands to the needy.
PROVERBS 31:20

136

Beware of the half truth. You may have gotten hold of the wrong half.

Give your servant a discerning heart.

1 KINGS 3:9

137

He who accepts evil, without protesting it, is really cooperating with it.

I will have nothing to do with evil.

PSALM 101:4

Never be afraid to trust an unknown future to a known God.

I will turn the darkness into light before them and make the rough places smooth.

ISAIAH 42:16

139

CLASS OF
2007

The only time you should be a passenger in life is when you know God is the One behind the wheel.

And thine ears shall hear a word behind thee, saying, This is the way, walk ye in it, when ye turn to the right hand, and when ye turn to the left.

ISAIAH 30:21 KJV

Where fear is present, wisdom cannot be.

The LORD is my light and my salvation—whom shall I fear?

PSALM 27:1

To see a world in a grain of sand and a heaven in a wildflower, hold infinity in the palm of your hand and eternity in an hour.

[God] has not left himself without testimony: He has shown kindness by giving you rain from heaven and crops in their seasons.

ACTS 14:17

142

When I despair, I remember
that all through history
the way of truth and love
has always won.

The Lord knows how to rescue godly men from trials.
2 PETER 2:9

143

No pain, no gain.

Consider it pure joy, my brothers, whenever you face trials of many kinds, because you know that the testing of your faith develops perseverance.

JAMES 1:2–3

Be what you wish others to become.

In everything set them an example by doing what is good.

TITUS 2:7

Before God created the universe, He already had you in mind.

The heavens declare the glory of God; the skies proclaim the work of his hands.

PSALM 19:1

CLASS OF 2007

Avoiding danger is no safer in the long run than outright exposure. Life is either a daring adventure, or nothing.

Alive, I'm Christ's messenger; dead, I'm his bounty.
Life versus even more life! I can't lose.
PHILIPPIANS 1:21 MSG

147

Every action of our lives touches on some chord that will vibrate in eternity.

In the same way, let your light shine before men, that they may see your good deeds and praise your Father in heaven.

Matthew 5:16

148

Faith is not merely you holding on to God—it is God holding on to you.

We live by faith, not by sight.

2 CORINTHIANS 5:7

149

Leap, and the net will appear.

As for God, his way is perfect; the word of the LORD is tried: he is a buckler to all them that trust in him.

2 SAMUEL 22:31 KJV

What God does,
He does well.

*I praise you because I am fearfully and wonderfully made;
your works are wonderful.*

PSALM 139:14

You can preach a better sermon with your life than with your lips.

Even I, the Messiah, am not here to be served, but to help others, and to give my life as a ransom for many.

MARK 10:45 TLB

152

Rare as is true love, true friendship is still rarer.

I have called you friends, for everything that I learned from my Father I have made known to you.

JOHN 15:15

There is no right way to do the wrong thing.

There is a way that seems right to a man, but in the end it leads to death.

PROVERBS 14:12

Believe in something larger than yourself.

Now faith is the substance of things hoped for, the evidence of things not seen.

HEBREWS 11:1 KJV

155

Honesty is the first chapter of the book of wisdom.

You deserve honesty from the heart; yes, utter sincerity and truthfulness.
Oh, give me this wisdom.

PSALM 51:6 TLB

CLASS OF 2007

What the caterpillar calls the end of the world, the Master calls a butterfly.

We, who with unveiled faces all reflect the Lord's glory,
are being transformed into his likeness with ever-increasing glory.

2 CORINTHIANS 3:18

157

God will not demand more from you than you can do. Whatever God asks of you, He will give you the strength to do.

So now, go. I am sending you to Pharaoh to bring my people the Israelites out of Egypt.

Exodus 3:10

Acknowledgments

We acknowledge and thank the following people for the quotes used in this book: Eleanor Roosevelt (4), Anatole France (5), Lao-Tsu (6), Bob Newhart (7), Colin Urquhart (8), Norman Vincent Peale (10), Jeremy Taylor (12), Ernest Hemingway (13), Arthur C. Clarke (14), Charles R. Swindoll (15), Lawrence J. Peter (17), Charles Spurgeon (18), Japanese Proverb (19), Joyce Meyers (20), Lucius Annaeus Seneca (21, 49), Phaedrus (22), A. Sachs (23), Plato (24), Franklin Delano Roosevelt (25), Olivia Leigh (26), Alexander Graham Bell (27), Karl Ludwig von Knebel (28), Tiorio (31), Napoleon Hill (32), Charlotte Brontë (33), Dorothy Bernard (34), Peter Marshall (35), Blaise Pascal (36), Erwin W. Lutzer (37, 68, 91, 147), Victor Hugo (38, 62), Petrarch (39), John Taylor (41), Paul Valéry (42), William Shedd (44), Oprah Winfrey (45), Denis Waitley (46), Archbishop Fulton J. Sheen (47), Daniel Webster (48), Maria von Trapp (50), Soren Kierkegaard (51), Oscar Wilde (52), Gene Fowler (53), Louisa May Alcott (55), Tennessee Williams (56), Wilfred A. Peterson (57), Martha Washington (58), Desiderius Erasmus (59), Andrew Jackson (60), Dorothy Dix (61), Horace (62), Elton Trueblood (63), Benjamin Franklin (64), Philip James Bailey (65), Henry Ward Beecher (66), Edmund Burke (67), Publilius Syrus (69), Tyron Edwards (70), Beth Moore (71, 128), A. W. Tozer (72), John Wesley (74, 75), Arnold Glasgow (76), Montaigne (77), Thomas Chalmers (78), Nicholas Caussin (79), Suetonius (80), Kay Arthur (82), Mark Twain (83), Oswald Chambers (84), Hannah Whitall Smith (85), Isak Dinesen (86), Eldridge Cleaver (87), Baruch Spinoza (88), A. J. Gossip (89), Louise Drisoll (90), Dwight L. Moody (93), Thomas Fuller (94), John Henry Newman (95), Ralph Waldo Emerson (97, 104, 124), John Ruskin (98) Ruth E. Renkel (99), Samuel Johnson (100, 133), Matthew Henry (103), George Bush (105), Henrietta Cornelia Mears (106), Dorothea Brande (107), Gregory of Nyssa (108), John Bunyan (109), Neil Anderson (110), Oliver Goldsmith (112, 127, 152), Albert Einstein (113, 134), Han Suyin (114), Pablo Casals (115), Henrik Ibsen (116), Saint Augustine of Hippo (117, 125), Jean François Regnard (118), Josiah Gilbert Holland (119), English Proverb (120), Leo Buscaglia (121), Steven Pagent (122), Hunter S. Thompson (123), Saint John Chrysostom (126), Earl Riney (129), Martin Luther King Jr. (131, 138), Jean Houston (132), Greg Anderson (135), Corrie ten Boom (139), Lucius C. Lactantius (141), William Blake (142), Mahatma Gandhi (143), Helen Keller (147), Edwin Hubbel Chapin (148), John Burroughs (150), Paul Johannes Oskar Tillich (151), Jean de La Fontaine (153), François Duc de La Rochefoucauld (154), Barbara Bush (155), Thomas Jefferson (156), Richard Bach (157), William Frederick Halsey Jr. (158).